W9-AUI-789

WHY DOGS DO THAT

WHY DOGS DO THAT

A COLLECTION OF CURIOUS CANINE BEHAVIORS

BY TOM DAVIS

WILLOW CREEK PRESS®

© 2013 Tom Davis

All Rights reserved. No part of this book may be reproduced or transmitted in any form by any means, electronic or mechanical, including photocopying, recording, or by any information storage and retrieval system, without written permission from the Publisher.

Published by Willow Creek Press, Inc.
P.O. Box 147, Minocqua, Wisconsin 54548

All illustrations © Peter Ring
All photos © agefotostock.com and their photographers except on page 26, 92, 122 © istockphoto.com and their photographers

Printed in China

CONTENTS

PREFACE

For as long as there have been dogs—15,000 years, give or take a few millennia—humans have been trying to figure out why they do the things they do. This is faintly ironic, given the fact that the dog is, in a very real sense, our handiwork, the product of our incessant tinkering with the machinery of nature. The thing that makes dogs so fascinating, and yet so perplexing, is that at times they seem almost human—and at other times they seem utterly alien. Author Edith Wharton referred to this dichotomy as the "us-ness" and "not-usness" with which every dog is endowed. We have made the dog in our own image, and we see reflected there the qualities that we'd like to think we possess: loyalty, courage, perseverance, compassion, selflessness, generosity, an astonishing capacity to love. As James Thurber, who understood dogs as well as anyone, put it, "If I have any beliefs about immortality, it is that certain dogs I have known will go to heaven, and very, very, few persons."

Trouble is, beneath its human veneer a dog is still a dog, with the same basic needs, urges, and instincts as the wolves from which it is descended (and with which, genetically speaking, it remains virtually identical). This is why we find so many aspects of canine behavior puzzling—and occasionally appalling. For example, the average person who considers his or her dog a member of the family is hard-pressed to reconcile its obvious relish for carrion, excrement, etc. The sexual indiscriminateness of most dogs also tends to give pet owners pause.

The problem, or course, is that we fall into the trap of applying human values to canine behavior. We "anthropomorphize," to use a word much bandied about these days. Viewed from a clear-eyed evolutionary perspective, however, most of the things dogs do make perfect sense. In the wild, where survival is the bottom line, any behavior that furthered the cause was eventually incorporated at the genetic level. It became instinctive, in other words, and while humans have selectively refined, augmented, and/or toned down these instincts to suit their own purposes, there is a cluster of core behaviors that all dogs, no matter how dissimilar they appear or how unrelated their intended function, have in common. A pointer may

point, a retriever may retrieve, a sled dog may pull, and a hound may follow a scent trail in full cry. At heart, though, they're all a lot more alike than they are different.

Why Dogs Do That is a humble attempt at fitting together some of the pieces of the canine puzzle. The book is meant to be both enlightening and entertaining, meaning that the reader is required to exercise a certain amount of old-fashioned common sense in separating the factual (or what is at least the prevailing opinion) from the tongue-in-cheek. Sticklers for scientific exactitude will no doubt find many of the explanations wanting. Well, so be it. This book is for the general interest reader and dog lover, not the specialist, and anyone who cites it to support his or her academic agenda is definitely barking up the wrong tree. The hope is that the reader will come away with a better understanding of what makes dogs tick, a deeper appreciation of the qualities that endear them to us, and, most important of all, a renewed commitment to according them the care, respect, and devotion they so richly deserve.

Laughter is encouraged, too.

WHY DO MALE DOGS LIFT THEIR LEGS?

Well, for one thing, if they stood on all fours, the way pups do (and the way adult dogs will sometimes do in situations of pressing urgency), they'd run the risk of splashing themselves on the backs of their forelegs. This is definitely uncool—sort of the canine equivalent of what happens to certain men when they're not paying attention to business, and as they go to zip up discover that they've rained on their trousers. More to the point, though, when a male dog lifts his leg he's in essence leaving his calling card.

While there may be an element of territoriality involved, "This is my turf, man," it's primarily a social gesture, a way of announcing to other dogs "I was here." In canine society as in human, it's important to stay in circulation, frequent the trendiest fire hydrants, etc. And, reminiscent of the contests in which young boys so gleefully engage, there's a bit of one-upmanship (updogship?) in the way every leg-lifter tries to make his mark just a tad higher than the last passerby. This can result in some truly awesome displays of balance, flexibility, and marksmanship.

WHY DO PUPPIES SOMETIMES CRY OUT EVEN WHEN NOTHING'S WRONG?

The kicker here is the qualifier "even when nothing's wrong." While there may be nothing obviously wrong—the puppy's not hungry, or cold, or being tormented by a littermate, or in a strange environment away from its mama, its siblings, and everything it's ever known—you have to remember that a young puppy is learning as it goes. With just about every moment that passes (every conscious one, anyway) it's exposed to new sensations and stimuli. A little puppy has essentially zero "life experience," and as a result everything comes as a surprise to it, sometimes so much so that the pup's startled into crying out. It could be a growl emanating from its own stomach, the bubble of a burp rising in its esophagus, a gassy twinge in its bowels, or just some neuron firing randomly and unexpectedly.

It could be something external, too, such as a noise (even one that doesn't strike us as loud), flipping on a light—literally anything, from within or without, that the puppy doesn't know what to make of, or that upsets its delicate status quo. Certainly some puppies are innately more "reactive" than others; it's one of the breeder's jobs to raise the pups in the kind of nurturing, stimulating environment that provides them with the confidence and "social skills" to adapt to new situations, overcome its fears, and ameliorate any neurotic tendencies. The last thing any breeder wants is to have a puppy from his/her kennel become one of Cesar Millan's case studies.

WHY DO DOGS DIG HOLES?

To fully understand canine behavior, you have to remember that if you scratch a dog, you find beneath the surface, a wolf. Advances in DNA analysis have proved that the dog is not only descended from the wolf, but is in fact a wolf subspecies—hence the revision of the dog's taxonomic classification from Canis familiaris to Canis lupus familiaris (the wolf is Canis lupus). Over the millions of years of the wolf's existence, digging—to excavate dens, extract hidden prey, or simply create a cool place to lie down—became an instinctive behavior, a survival skill hard-wired into the genetic circuitry. In other words, dogs, which have been around for a mere 15,000 years or so, dig—whether we want them to or not. It's often a symptom of boredom, something like the sundry destructive behaviors exhibited by kids when the little angels have "nothing better to do."

As a footnote, the digging ability of terriers, breeds developed in the British Isles specifically to hunt "ground game" such as badgers, foxes, otters, etc., was one of the qualities for which they were originally prized, qualities that caused them to be known in antiquity as "earth dogges." A contemporary homeowner surveying the cratered ruins of his or her backyard is likely to call them by other, more colorful, names.

WHY DO PUPPIES HAVE DEWCLAWS?

Down in the swamps and canebrakes, there are backwoodsmen who swear on Stonewall Jackson's grave that a dog born with dewclaws on its hind legs is "natch'ral snakeproof"—immune to the effects of a venomous snakebite, that is. And they'll back up this claim by trotting out a rawboned hound, showing you the curved, thumb-like claws on the inside of its hind legs, and telling you that the dog's been snakebit more than once but that the dewclaws "sucked up the poison."

Essentially a fifth toe that occupies a position on the canine foot analogous to the human thumb, the dewclaw is a remnant from a time in the distant past—as in over 40 million years ago—when the dog's ancestors climbed trees. Having five toes was an advantage then, but as these proto-canids evolved into a ground-dwelling species that relies on its speed and agility afoot to capture prey, the fifth toe became redundant and, over time, receded to become the vestigial digit it is today. It's not uncommon for the dewclaw to be completely absent from the hind legs of many breeds, although there are a few—notably the Great Pyrenees and the Briard—that have a double set of hind dewclaws. Claims of snakeproofing aside, the question of whether dewclaws serve any useful purpose, whether they pose a potential hazard (inadvertently scratching a cornea, for example, or catching and tearing on obstructions), and whether they should be removed shortly after whelping (when it's a simple and relatively painless procedure) continue to be hotly debated by dog folk.

HOW CAN PUPPIES FROM THE SAME LITTER HAVE DIFFERENT SIRES?

This sort of gives new meaning to the phrase "Who's your daddy?" All kidding aside, this is for real. It can happen, and it does—although ethical, conscientious breeders try very hard to see that it doesn't. The technical term for this phenomenon by the way is "superfecundation."

There are a variety of factors that allow it to occur, the most obvious being that female dogs produce multiple ova (eggs). This is the reason dogs have litters of puppies rather than individual ones. Yeah, I know, duh. But it's somewhat more complicated than that. When dogs ovulate the ova, or oocytes, are still immature. They don't become fully mature until two and one-half to three days following ovulation (although they're capable of being penetrated by sperm during this period), and they remain viable for two to seven days after that. Canine sperm can remain viable in the reproductive tract for up to eight days… So you do the math. The bottom line is that because (A) dogs are polygamous breeders, and (B) females remain receptive to males for a week or more, the sperm of multiple sires can potentially find itself in position to uphold the family honor.

So who is your daddy?

WHY DO FEMALE DOGS SQUAT?

Actually, not all of them do—or at least not all of them do all of the time. Quite a few females, particularly those with dominant personality traits, lift their legs as boldly and assertively as their male counterparts. And females in season will lift their leg to help "advertise" their availability.

It must be admitted, however, that they rarely attain the lofty heights (nor exhibit the triumphant arcs) of which the male is capable. It's a simple matter of anatomy, the same reason boys write their names in the snow and girls don't. Canine or human, there's no getting around the fact that the male is better-equipped for directional urination—a dubious claim to fame, perhaps, but hey, we'll take it.

WHY DO DOGS BARK INCESSANTLY WHEN TIED UP OR CLOSELY CONFINED?

Dogs bark for a variety of reasons: to express fear, aggression, or excitement, to sound a warning, to invite other dogs to play, the list goes on. In the case of the dog that's tied up or confined to a small area, barking is often a symptom of boredom and/or general discontentment. Frankly, many dogs that are kept in such conditions have been poorly socialized, and receive very little attention, affection, and "quality time" that make dogs well-adjusted citizens. Also, as the dog's "territory" shrinks, it feels exposed and insecure, growing increasingly sensitive to the perception of threat.

Years ago, an insurance company terminated my homeowner's policy because one of my setters barked unceasingly at the inspector they'd dispatched to look things over. I was living in the country at the time, and my dogs were staked to chains that allowed them to comfortably enter their wooden houses, but restricted their movements to a circumscribed radius. Unannounced, the insurance man, a total stranger, was not warmly greeted by old Zack (who didn't have a mean bone in his body). He probably wouldn't have been so vociferous if he'd had the luxury of a fenced run. (For the record, an insurance company with a keener understanding of canine psychology was happy to provide me with coverage.)

WHY DO DOGS CHASE CARS?

All dogs, to one degree or another chase. It's instinctive, a manifestation of the "prey drive" without which their wild forebears could not have survived. Something moves, and the wolf—or the untrained dog—chases it. This genetically programmed response to motion is what makes a weasel, for example, kill every chicken in the henhouse. It's not that the weasel's "bloodthirsty;" rather, it's simply reacting in the way it has evolved to react.

Some canine behaviorists have gone so far as to suggest that dogs chase cars because they "mistake" them for the large wild ungulates, such as moose, that constitute such a significant percentage of the wolf's prey base. It's certainly true that a moose is as big as a lot of cars, and, drawing another parallel, it's equally true that moose wound, maim, and even kill their fair share of wolves. The flip side of this coin is that some wolf-moose encounters end successfully, at least from the wolf's perspective. The same cannot be said of the typical dog-car encounter, to which the only happy ending is a dog that escapes injury and, you hope, learns a lesson it will never forget.

WHY DO RETRIEVING BREED PUPPIES RETRIEVE AT A VERY EARLY AGE?

The old professional trainer was putting on a brave front, but we both knew he was nearing the end of the line. Now, as he shuffled toward a dusty shelf in the dimly lit kennel building, a pair of weanling Labrador retriever pups—one yellow, one black—nipped at his pants legs. He found a puppy-sized dummy to which he'd duct-taped a pair of pigeon wings, waved it in the youngsters' faces to get their attention, and tossed it down the hallway. The floppy-eared pups, still at that age when they seem to have more skin than they can fill, scrabbled after it. The yellow one got there first, and without missing a beat she grabbed the dummy, turned around, and brought it back. The old trainer beamed— and the years fell away. Through the simple act of retrieving, a pudgy little puppy had given an old man reason enough to carry on.

Perhaps she had not made him young again, but she'd helped him to remember how it felt.

What made this magic possible? Selective breeding—generation upon generation of it. By choosing sires and dams who exhibit a strong natural inclination to retrieve, and repeating this process over literally dozens of generations and hundreds of years, the retrieving instinct has been intensified until it burns in the Lab, the golden, and the Chesapeake like the focused blue flame of a welder's torch. It's their dominant, defining characteristic; they're never happier than when they're retrieving, and they'll pester you unmercifully to get you to throw something— anything—for them to fetch. They can't help it; they were born that way.

WHY ARE PUPPIES BORN WITH THEIR EYES CLOSED?

All mammals have evolved complex "strategies" for reproduction, gestation, and development that, given the environmental conditions that have shaped them and the ecological niche they occupy, optimize their chances for survival and perpetuation of the species. In the whitetailed deer, for example, the gestation period is fairly long—about six and one-half months—but the fawns are very precocious, able to stand, walk, see, hear, and respond to danger within minutes of birth.

The various canines have taken a somewhat different tack. The gestation period in dogs is only about two months—58 to 63 days, on average—the trade-off being that the puppies are not nearly as far along as the young of some other species. Newborn puppies are, in fact, helpless; you could almost say that while not technically premature, they're in a sense neo-natal. The basic reason that puppies are born with their eyelids tightly shut, then, is that the eye itself is still developing. It's extremely fragile, needing all the protection it can get not only from from foreign objects (grit, dirt, etc.) and potential pathogens but from bright light that could damage the eye's delicate photoreceptors and optic mechanisms. Even so, an occasional pup contracts an eye infection in utero from its mother, and because it's so difficult (if not impossible) to detect any symptoms with the eyes clamped shut, loss of vision, and loss of the eye itself, are real possibilities.

Most puppies begin to open their eyes at about two weeks of age, although several more weeks must elapse before their eyes, and their eyesight, are fully developed.

WHY DO DOGS INSIST ON SLEEPING IN BED WITH YOU?

What self-respecting dog would choose to sleep on the floor when there's a warm, soft, comfortable bed available? It would be like turning down champagne for club soda, or lobster thermidor for tuna surprise. Plus, in the context of the pack dynamic, the dog that's allowed to sleep with its alpha male and/or female feels as if it's climbed another rung on the social ladder. It's a kind of privileged access, like scoring a backstage pass to a Rolling Stones concert.

Of course, some dogs get a little greedy after they've had a taste of this pleasure, and begin to consider you the bed guest. You haven't really experienced sleeplessness until you've had to contort yourself around a dog that's claimed the center of the mattress and absolutely refuses to move. Dogs also snore, have convulsive dreams, and indulge in middle-of-the-night licking frenzies. In other words, letting your dog sleep with you is not necessarily a bed of roses.

WHY DO PUPPIES SLEEP IN A PILE?

For the same reason that you snuggle under the blankets with your honey on a cold winter's night: warmth. (If you were thinking of something else, you must be a newlywed.) Puppies in their "neo-natal" stage—their first two weeks or life, roughly—lack the ability to regulate or maintain their core temperature, which gradually rises from about 97°F at birth to the "normal" 101°F at about three weeks of age. They're completely dependent on their environment for warmth during this period; conversely, they're extremely susceptible to cold. This is the reason conscientious breeders always provide some kind of supplemental heat source to the whelping pen. A heated pad is one popular option (with care taken to see it doesn't get too hot); another is a heat lamp suspended—at a safe remove, obviously—over the puppies' "nest." It doesn't have to be like a sauna—there's the puppies' mama to consider, too—but it should be on the upper side of comfortable.

Of course, the closest and most accessible sources of heat in the environment of a typical puppy are its littermates, hence the familiar "pile o' pups" as one after the other crawls, climbs, and worms his or her way onto the stack. It's sort of the same principle that we use when we create a nice, neat mound of charcoal briquets preparatory to carbonizing a perfectly good piece of beef. Truth be told, though, these puppy pile-ups can be an indication that the ambient temperature's a bit too low, forcing the pups to go to extremes to conserve warmth.

WHY DO DOGS MOUNT YOUR GUEST'S LEG?

This behavior, which is most often seen in younger dogs (although some friends of mine had a middle-aged Bassett that was incorrigible in this respect), is nature's way of preparing them for the Real Thing. Practice makes perfect, in other words. Some females—again, generally younger ones—will hump your leg too, almost as if they're trying to sort out their sexual identity. A few never do; or should I say, in this era of political correctness, that they "choose an alternative lifestyle," homosexual behavior among dogs being more common than you might suspect.

WHY ARE PUPPIES' EYES ALWAYS BLUE WHEN THEY FIRST OPEN THEM?

Again, it comes back to the fact that at the time they begin to open, usually at about two weeks of age, the puppy's eyes are still immature. In this instance, the pigment in the iris—the "colored" portion of the eye—remains undeveloped. And in much the same way that the shorter wavelengths of sunlight are "scattered" by molecules in the atmosphere to produce the appearance of blue sky—"Rayleigh scattering," this is called, after the English physicist who first described it in the 1870s—light entering the lightly pigmented iris scatters, reflects, and appears to our eyes as some shade of blue. A milky, grayish-blue is typical, but some puppy's eyes appear ice blue, while others are almost green. As the pigment "fills in" over the following weeks and months, the eyes of most puppies grow darker, ultimately becoming whatever hue, from pale yellow gold to nearly black, the palette of genetic inheritance has painted for them. The exceptions are those breeds, such as Siberian huskies and Australian shepherds, in which blue eyes are common; in these instances, the level of dark pigment remains low, producing the blue "effect."

To put it another way: The color blue is not inherent in the eye—there's no blue pigment—but a function of the way it's "singled out" from the spectrum of visible light.

WHY DO PUPPIES LOVE TO BITE ONE ANOTHER ON THE EARS AND THE BACK OF THE NECK?

The term "rough and tumble" might have been coined with puppies in mind. It certainly describes their world to the proverbial T, filled as it is with surprise attacks, tag-team wrestling matches, and tussles of every description. Sometimes a clear victor emerges, but more often the pups simply collapse as one under the weight of their exertions, wobbling like drunks for a moment or two before passing out as instantaneously and comprehensively as if they'd been conked on the head with a sap.

In the same way that the Battle of Waterloo was won on the playing fields of Eton, as Lord Wellington famously observed, "play fighting" prepares puppies to handle themselves in the cold, cruel world. (It was a lot more important when dogs were still wolves, but deep inside every dog there's a voice telling it not to take its next meal for granted.) It helps them develop coordination, motor skills, and overall physical soundness, and it also nurtures confidence and independence. As far as why the ears and the back of the neck absorb the brunt of the punishment, I think it's largely a matter of opportunity: they're soft, they're easy to get a good grip on, and while the "recipient" may scream bloody murder the chances of actually drawing blood are remote. In fact, I have a hunch that one of the reasons puppies gravitate to these areas is precisely because they're resistant to injury—nature's way of letting the little buggers have at it tooth and nail without doing any lasting harm. Play fighting also teaches puppies how to control their biting behavior, so they can later hold in reserve for only the direst emergencies.

WHY DO DOGS BURY BONES?

Essentially, dogs bury bones for the same reason squirrels bury nuts: as a hedge against the lean times. Not that the typical dog has to worry about where his next meal will come from, but his wild ancestors figured out a long time ago that when food is easy to come by, it's a good idea to put some aside— kind of like setting up a savings account that can be drawn on in an emergency. This behavior is called "caching," and it's common among wolves and certain species of foxes as well as dogs. (When I find it necessary to feed my dogs in their travel crates during hunting trips, my English setter female will "cache" any leftovers by very carefully covering her bowl with a layer of straw.)

My impression, though, judging by the prevalence of the theme in the popular art, literature, and film (including cartoons) of the early and mid-20th century, is that dogs aren't burying bones the way they used to. Not that they're any less interested; the more likely explanation is that they're simply not getting the opportunity, the veterinary profession having done a pretty thorough job educating dog owners about the consequences of a shard of bone lodging in their pet's digestive tract. The jaws of the average dog, after all, can generate several hundred pounds per square inch of crushing force, more than enough to splinter even the toughest beef bone.

WHY ARE SOME PUPPIES "RUNTS?"

Everyone is familiar with the phrase "the runt of the litter," whether they've ever laid eyes on a litter of puppies or not. In canine legend of course the runt, after being passed over in favor of his larger, more promising littermates (and enduring all manner of cruel misfortunes), grows up to fight man-eating grizzlies and rescue avalanche victims from certain death. There may be a germ of truth to this stereotype. Some believe that the runt, because it has to fight harder to nurse and get its rightful share in general, develops an extra measure of tenacity and determination.

What makes a runt a runt? Often it's simply an expression of normal genetic variation— the luck of the draw, in other words. A few pups are larger, most are somewhere in the middle, and a few are smaller. This gets into semantics, and the question of whether the smallest pup in the litter is always, by definition, "the runt"—even if it's just fractionally smaller than its littermates— or if "runt" refers only to puppies that are conspicuously smaller than the rest. Be that as it may, another reason some puppies lag behind in the size derby is that, due to the placement of the placenta, they don't receive as much nourishment through their umbilical cord as their littermates do. Some puppies may be conceived later too, giving their littermates what amounts to a head start. It may take a while, but these pups usually catch up and develop normally.

Some runts, however, owe their small size to a serious underlying medical condition. This is why, if you have your heart set on the runt of the litter, you should be sure that it appears healthy and shows no signs of abnormal behavior (extreme timidity, for example), and have it thoroughly examined by a vet before any money changes hands.

WHY DO DOGS LICK THEMSELVES, AND OTHER DOGS?

Among other reasons, dogs lick to cleanse themselves, facilitate the healing of wounds, and soothe skin irritations. Licking can also be an expression of boredom or nervousness, the result of which is often a knobby sore on the carpal joint (the dog's "wrist") called a "lick granuloma."

Dams lick their puppies to clean them (thus removing scent that could be detected by predators) and stimulate breathing and elimination. Males lick the vulvas of females to evaluate their receptivity to breeding (sort of the canine equivalent of foreplay); females lick the penises of males to determine who they've been sleeping with, so to speak. Dogs lick one another out of affection, playfulness, deference ("Lick my boots, knave!"), and occasionally for the simple reason that there's something good to eat—a salty "eye booger," for example—clinging to the other dog's coat.

WHY ARE SOME LITTERS VERY UNIFORM IN SIZE AND APPEARANCE WHILE OTHERS ARE ALL OVER THE PLACE?

t's an amazing thing, the way the puppies in one litter will resemble the proverbial peas in a pod, while the puppies in another litter suggest the vegetable medley: peas, carrots, corn, green beans, maybe even some broccoli and cauliflower. Generally speaking, though, the more alike in size and appearance the parents, the more uniform in size and appearance the pups. At the risk of mixing metaphors, the apple doesn't fall far from the tree. In this same vein, purebred litters tend to be more uniform than mixed-breed litters, because what makes purebreds purebreds is that much of the variability has been weeded out in favor of specific characteristics that have been "fixed" over time by selective breeding. The result is what biologists call homozygosity, which is a fancy way of saying that dogs of the same breed have similar genetic material. Breed

two Labradors, and their pups won't look like Schnauzers. This effect is intensified when you breed within an established bloodline, a practice known as linebreeding or, in a more extreme form, inbreeding. The legendary Elhew pointers, a strain cultivated for over 60 years by the late Robert G. Wehle, were perhaps the apotheosis of this, breeding "true to type" generation after generation.

Mate dogs of different breeds, however, and all bets are off. Now you're dealing with heterozygosity, which basically means that the gene pool resembles one of those frat house concoctions in which everyone brings a bottle and pours it into the bathtub. You never know what you'll get—which is why a single litter can have wildly different looking pups.

WHY DO DOGS EAT VILE THINGS LIKE HORSE APPLES AND COW PIES?

Animals in general are not plagued by the Fear of Excrement that haunts humankind. Many winter birds—wild turkeys, for example—depend on the "hot lunch program": cow manure which they pick through for kernels of undigested grain and other tasty nuggets. Other species practice "self-recycling," routinely ingesting their own scat. Rabbits literally must consume their own feces to obtain certain vitamins critical to their survival. Dogs eat horse apples, cow pies, and the like because their wild ancestors, rather than dying of starvation when normal fare couldn't be found, adapted to eating anything that had nutritive value, including excreta. In this regard, think of wolves—and, therefore, dogs—as carnivores by nature, but omnivores by necessity.

Of course, there's probably nothing more repulsive than the sight of an adored pet—the same animal that frenziedly licks your face, given the chance—gobbling its own stools, or those of its kennelmates. (The technical term for this behavior, by the way, is "coprophagy.") Dogs are great imitators, and it's believed that one of the reasons they do this is to imitate what they observe you doing when you pick up after them. And because dogs pick things up with their mouths, the rest comes more or less naturally. Ironically, the tremendous improvements in the quality of dog food over the past decade or so have, in all likelihood, made this behavior even more common.

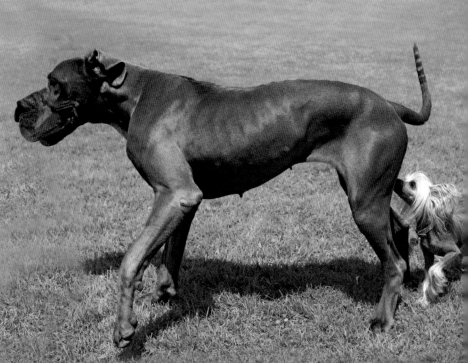

WHY DO DOGS SNIFF THE BEHINDS OF OTHER DOGS?

The long and short of it is that this is how dogs identify and introduce themselves to one another, having found it extremely difficult—and not particularly enlightening—to shake hands and exchange the usual pleasantries. A dog sniffing another dog's "inguinal area," as the anatomical nether region is known, is essentially saying "Hello, who are you? Have we met before?"

Every dog has a unique scent "signature" created by the secretions of its anal sacs, a pair of small, kidney-shaped structures on either side of the anus. This signature not only serves to distinguish it from all other dogs, but apparently reveals whether the dog in question is male or female. And while scientists suspect that the scent signature relays additional information as well, they're still scratching their heads over exactly what that might be.

WHY DO DOGS LOVE US EVEN AFTER PUNISHMENT, OR WHEN WE'VE LET THEM DOWN?

Because the love of a dog is almost wholly unconditional. There are no strings attached, no riders or special stipulations; there's no fine print, no expiration date, no statute of limitations. They love to a depth and degree that few of us, I fear, reciprocate, and if we're quick to forgive them, they're even quicker to forgive us. Their love is of an order that we probably don't deserve, and when we know that we have wronged them, acting out of anger or ignorance or sheer stupidity, their unwavering devotion shames us. There is nothing on this earth more heart-rending, more awful, than the pleading look in the eyes of a dog that cannot understand why the person it loves to the very marrow has caused it pain.

Why dogs should so single us out for favor, giving in vastly greater proportion to what they receive in return, is a question that really can't be answered. It defies all logical explanation—and yet it explains everything, too, because when you strip away the intervening layers, it is this fierce, abiding, unconditional love that ultimately defines Dog. It is also why the dog, of all the creatures that inhabit this chaotic ark, is the one most surely infused by the spark of the divine.

WHY DO DOGS CHASE THEIR TAILS?

Because they're there, of course. Watch a dog as it chases its tail, and you can almost hear it thinking, "What is this thing that keeps following me around, and why can't I catch it?" Quantifying canine intelligence is a very tricky business; there are dogs that display great aptitude for obedience work yet don't have the sense to come in out of the rain, and dogs that are seemingly untrainable yet exhibit astonishing reasoning and decision-making powers.

It's a pretty safe bet, though, that a dog that persists in chasing its tail wasn't at the front of the line when the brains were being distributed—although, in fairness to the dog, prolonged and repeated tail chasing can also be symptomatic of seizures brought on by a serious epileptic-type disorder. If your pet exhibits such behavior, get it to a veterinarian, pronto.

WHY DO PUPPIES HAVE SUCH SHARP TEETH?

"My, what sharp teeth you have!" exclaimed Little Red Riding Hood to the Big Bad Wolf, who you'll recall was posing as Red's grandmother at the time. Dogs, of course, are essentially domesticated wolves—their DNA is all but identical—and perhaps the single biggest thing we can do to help make sense of our dogs, their behaviors, and their physical and psychological characteristics is to keep this wolfy ancestry in mind. As I like to put it: scratch a dog, find a wolf.

The teeth of puppies offer a prime example. When you think about the conditions in which a female wolf raises her pups, it becomes pretty obvious that their needle-sharp choppers, which begin to come in at around three weeks of age, serve a variety of critically important purposes. One is that they facilitate weaning. We all have nipples, and if you can imagine those tiny daggers clamping down on yours... well, I think you get the point. Once intense pain becomes part of the equation, Mama Wolf's ready to kick 'em out the door, where they can begin the process of learning to fend for themselves. (Too bad there isn't as powerful an incentive for human mothers to give the boot to their slacker, video game-addicted offspring.) By the same token, the weanling wolf needs good teeth in order to feed on the prey animals (or pieces of animals) that its dam retrieves to the den. Because the pup lacks size and strength, its teeth have to be that much sharper in order for it to tear off chunks of meat. By the time it cuts its adult teeth at six months of age, this is no longer an issue.

The adult teeth also have to last a lifetime, so they're necessarily sturdier and less bayonet-like.

All of which is to say that the reason puppies have such sharp teeth is because they proved useful to their wild ancestors in the struggle for survival.

WHY DO PUPPIES ALWAYS WANT TO GET TO YOUR FACE?

One of the keys to understanding canine behavior is that the dog's primary means of taking in the world around it is its sense of smell. What makes this a difficult concept for us to wrap our minds around is that we, too, have a sense of smell, and we naturally try to put ourselves in our dogs' place by imagining what it would be like if ours was better. Except it doesn't work that way; our imaginations aren't that good. The dog's nose is so vastly superior to ours, so much more powerful and discerning, that it might as well be a different organ entirely, one that allows the dog to operate in a realm of perception that's utterly closed to us. The only legitimate comparison—the only one that frames the discussion in truly meaningful terms—is between the dog's sense of smell and our sense of sight. This is why I like to say that dogs see with their noses.

The same goes for puppies. In fact, it's tempting to speculate that, within the intricate calculus of evolution, one of the reasons puppies are born blind and deaf is that it forces them to rely on their noses first, foremost, and forever. The reason they love to get to our faces, then, is that they can drink in the incredible bouquet of aromas emanating from our mouths (and clinging to our lips, mustaches, etc.). It's a curious thing about dogs that they appear to enjoy our breath—morning breath, beer breath, it doesn't seem to matter—and if that doesn't illustrate the fact that they smell things a whole lot differently than we do, I don't know what does.

WHY DO ADULT DOGS CHEW ON BONES, RUGS, ANTIQUES, ETC.?

This is really a two-part question. All dogs, their age notwithstanding, chew on bones; that's simply a given. In evolutionary terms, bone-gnawing no doubt became instinctive because the wolves that indulged in it, even after every molecule of meat was gone, kept their teeth and gums healthier, longer, and thus gained an advantage in the struggle for survival. Rugs, antiques, and the like are a somewhat different matter (although there is a certain indiscriminateness at the heart of the chewing impulse).

Assuming your dog knows better—one of the proverbial "big ifs"—chewing these off-limits items probably reflects its feeling that it isn't receiving enough attention. To paraphrase the famous remark made by Glenn Close's chilling character in *Fatal Attraction*, the typical dog will not be ignored—especially a house dog that's accustomed to lots of praise, petting and play. It's analogous to the child of inattentive or preoccupied parents who not only purposely commits some petty household crime but makes sure he gets caught. The way the kid—or the dog—sees it, it's better to risk a scolding than to remain invisible. Of course, there could also be a revenge factor involved, which would explain why your dog zeroes in unerringly on your most valuable piece of furniture.

WHY DO PUPPIES CHEW VIRTUALLY *EVERYTHING?*

Dogs of all ages are hard-wired to chew. In the wild (remember: scratch a dog, find a wolf), chewing on bones not only enabled the dog's ancestors to reap the nutritional benefit of every last molecule of protein but helped keep their teeth and gums healthy as well. Better health translates into a better chance to survive, which translates into a better chance to procreate… and in the evolutionary long run chewing became one of the definitive behaviors of the entire canine race.

Puppies, of course, chew for the added reason that it facilitates teething. The worst of it (from the standpoint of the typical homeowner, I mean) usually occurs when they're shedding their puppy teeth and cutting their permanent set. During this period, which begins at around three months of age and culminates at six to seven months,

pups literally chew everything. The legs of wooden furniture are a favored target—they tend to be at puppy level, for one thing, and the wood has a pleasing "mouth feel"— along with electrical cords, shoes and slippers (leather is as irresistible to puppies as beer nuts are to barflies), stuffed animals, pillows, rugs, the list goes on (and on).

Another reason puppies chew is the sheer thrill of finding out what they can do with them. It's no different when we get a new toy, or suddenly discover an aptitude, such as playing a musical instrument or whacking 300-yard drives, that we didn't know we possessed. Boredom tends to exacerbate problem chewing, and it also tends to be more prevalent in breeds like Labs and goldens that seem to have an innate need to use their mouths, whether for good, i.e., retrieving, or evil, i.e., shredding everything in sight.

WHY DO DOGS ROLL IN VILE THINGS LIKE DECAYING CARP?

There are a couple of theories, by no means mutually exclusive, that explain why dogs take such obvious and unabashed delight in rolling in stuff that makes us gag: excrement, carrion (the older and fouler, the better), anything and everything that is rotten, putrid, and deliquescent. And they don't just roll in it; wriggling joyfully on their backs, they do their damnedest to smear it around and rub it in. The more specific hypothesis suggests that dogs roll in stinky stuff to mask their own scent, and thus gain an edge over prey species (remember: scratch a dog, find a wolf) that might otherwise detect them and flee. (Contemporary human deer hunters do much the same thing when dousing their clothing with various bottled scents.)

The other theory, more general in application, holds that it's a way for a dog to tell other dogs where they've been and what they found there. A dog streaked with excrescence is viewed by his brethren as a storyteller, and canine society holds storytellers in high esteem. This much is certain: Old-time hound handlers and bird dog trainers agree that the dogs with the best noses are the ones most inclined to cover themselves in excrement. Given the fact that an average dog has some 220 million scent receptors (a human has a paltry 5 million), it really makes you wonder.

WHY DO RETRIEVING BREEDS RETRIEVE?

Virtually all dogs possess the retrieving instinct to some degree, the archetypal example being the dam who picks up a fugitive pup and "retrieves" it to the whelping pen. In the wild, of course, wolves retrieve small prey animals (or pieces of larger ones) for their young to feed upon. It's natural for dogs to pick things up in their mouths and carry them around—sticks, gloves, shed deer antlers, dead carp, etc.—and from there it's not a big step to get them to bring their booty to you. Praise and a tennis ball have probably taught more dogs to retrieve than any other method, ever.

What distinguishes the retrieving breeds—Labs, goldens, Chesapeakes, etc.—is their desire in this respect. If you want to get technical about it, this desire is a selective—i.e., human-induced—refinement of the basic prey drive; instead of taking the quarry (or its substitute) in its jaws and killing it, the retriever takes it in its jaws and tenderly (you hope) delivers it to hand. Dogs recognized as retrievers have existed since the 16th century (if not earlier); in the late-18th and early 19th centuries, the progenitor of the modern Lab was used on the high seas to retrieve fish that had become disentangled from the nets. By breeding one dog with a strong inclination to retrieve to another, the retrieving instinct was eventually "fixed," with the development of the specific breeds we know today not coming until later.

WHY DO POINTING BREEDS POINT?

When a mammalian predator stalks its prey, it typically "freezes" for a few moments before springing into action. This hesitation is at the root of the pointing instinct. While various hound-type dogs had been employed for millennia to successfully hunt and capture four-footed game, birds were a different story. Dogs could find them, but finding them usually meant putting them to wing. And unless you were a nobleman with a falcon, a flushed bird was a lost bird in those pre-firearm days. But some insightful soul observed that a few dogs occasionally hesitated, momentarily transfixed, when they encountered scent. If the dog could be trained to "set" its birds rather than flush them, a hunter might be able to sneak up and cast a net over them.

Indeed, the earliest written accounts of pointing dogs, dating to the 13th century, would seem to indicate that it was more a trained behavior then than an instinctive one. By the 16th century, however, when "fowling pieces" were beginning to come into widespread use, selective breeding had produced dogs with a pronounced natural tendency to point. By that time, too, the two basic divisions of pointing dogs had been established, with the shorthaired breeds known generically as "pointers" and the longhairs as "setters" or "setting dogges." At its best, the point not only indicates the presence and location of game, but has the effect of making it "hold" until deliberately flushed by the hunter.

WHY DO DOGS HAVE TO SMELL YOUR GUEST'S CROTCH?

This is a sort of corollary to the previous question. What you have to keep in mind is that to the average, well-socialized dog, humans are not different from them in kind, but only in degree—superior, albeit, from the dog's perspective, somewhat addled. Your dog considers you and your immediate family to be members of its pack, with each individual occupying a specific niche in the pack hierarchy. Typically, the dog assumes a subordinate role, although we're all familiar with households in which the dog rules the roost, as it were, having figured out that its people are either unable or unwilling to assert their dominance.

The upshot is that dogs sniff human crotches for the same reason they sniff canine rear ends: to establish identity. It's also likely that dogs are simply attracted by the bouquet of interesting aromas emanating from this region of the human body. A certain locational inevitability may be at work, too: All else equal, the muzzle of the average dog is carried at roughly the same level as the crotch of the average person.

WHY DO SOME PUPPIES BULLY THEIR LITTERMATES?

Well, because some puppies are bullies, the way some kids are. (Some adults are bullies, too, of course, including more than a few with addresses in Washington, D.C.) And just as two-legged bullies swagger, posture, cow their subordinates, and assert their real or imagined superiority at every opportunity, the four-legged kind take a snarky delight in lording over their littermates. They push their brothers and sisters around, commandeering their food, water, and toys and making it clear that what the others do have is only at the pleasure of the Tough Guy.

Unlike human bullies, however, whose behavior is typically explained by deep-rooted feelings of inferiority (if not by an intransigent meanness straight out of Cormac McCarthy), canine bullying is ultimately an expression of dominance aimed at establishing one's place in the hierarchy of the pack—although the worst bullies, ironically, are generally not the alpha dogs themselves but the alpha "wannabes," the pups whose reach exceeds their grasp. So it could be that an element of inferiority drives this behavior after all. Sometimes, too, a mild-mannered pup that's been quietly taking it from the bully will reach its breaking point, retaliate with startling fury, and in an instant reshuffle the whole nascent pack dynamic. You know what they say: It's not the size of the dog in the fight, but the size of the fight in the dog.

WHY DO DOGS CHASE CATS?

Because it's so dang much fun, that's why. While it's inaccurate to claim, as so many "authorities" have, that dogs and cats are "natural enemies," there's no doubt that the average dog takes a special delight in running a cat up a tree. After all, the cat is the Anti-Dog: insolent, untrustworthy, conniving, mercenary in its loyalties, heinously and repugnantly feline.

What dog worth its salt wouldn't try to put such a fiendish, irredeemable beast to rout, especially one that spits, hisses, arches its back debauchedly, and utters weird, unearthly moans? In this respect, the cat-chasing dog is merely fulfilling the destiny for which its forebears were domesticated 15,000 years ago: to serve mankind. The alternative explanation is that (A) dogs chase things (as noted previously) and (B) cats are handy.

WHY DO PUPPIES MAKE "PLAY" GROWLS BUT NOT "MEAN" GROWLS? WHEN DO THE "MEAN" GROWLS START?

Of the many puppy behaviors guaranteed to prompt a bemused chuckle, the "puppy growl" has to be near the top of the list. It's just so incongruous to hear this mock-ferocious sound issue from such a tiny, cuddly, utterly unthreatening source—something like being in the audience when a petite singer like Mariah Carey or Martina McBride takes the stage, opens her mouth, and all but blows the roof off. You wonder, 'Where the heck did that come from?'

Puppy growls are part-and-parcel of the whole "play fighting" ritual, the process by which puppies learn their capabilities in combat and, just as importantly, learn to control and inhibit them. The function of growling, in fact, is not merely to serve as a warning, but as a deterrent; in the wild, where these behaviors evolved and were incorporated into the dog's genetic blueprint, there's very little survival value in scrapping over every bone of contention. And while the pup doing the growling undoubtedly thinks he (or she) means business, puppy growls clearly lack the menacing tone of "mean" growls, the kind that make the hair on the back of your neck stand up, to say nothing of the hair on the backs of any dogs in the vicinity. Dogs will indulge in occasional bouts of play fighting throughout their lives (those that live as house- or kennel-mates in particular), but among littermates the play fighting period starts winding down at about 11 weeks of age and is pretty much over by 15 weeks. After that, the growls tend to have teeth in them.

WHY DO DOGS GULP THEIR FOOD RATHER THAN SAVOR IT?

To tell the truth, some dogs are dainty, finicky eaters—much to the consternation of their owners, who, in a role-reversing twist, often themselves assume the role of beggars, coaxing and cajoling their precious pet to take one more itsy-bitsy bite. In the main, however, it must be admitted that dogs display an appalling lack of table manners. They don't eat their food; they Hoover it, gobbling it up so fast and furiously that it's a wonder they don't black out for forgetting to breathe. (Whoever coined the term "chow hound" knew what they were talking about.)

But it isn't simply the rate of ingestion that's remarkable, it's the volume, too. Long before Beldar Conehead uttered the immortal words "Let us consume mass quantities," dogs were doing just that: They've been known to bolt as much as one-fifth of their body weight in food in a single belly-busting session. The explanation for this gluttonous behavior lies in the competition that occurs whenever "social carnivores"—i.e., wolves— bring down prey. If not exactly a case of winner-take-all and devil-take-the-hindmost, the animal that made quick work of feeding put itself in a better position to survive and pass along its genes. So when you accuse your dog of "wolfing down" its food, you're using precisely the right metaphor.

WHY DO SOME DOGS HOWL?

"Some" is definitely the operative word here. Some dogs howl frequently, even incessantly; some dogs howl rarely, or only when prompted by the howling of others; some dogs never seem to howl at all. I could get my old English setter, Zack, to howl simply by blowing a few plaintive notes on a cheap harmonica, and my impression is that male dogs are more inclined to howl than females.

It also has been observed that "wolfish" breeds—huskies, for example—tend to be particularly enthusiastic howlers. Dogs—like wolves, and like their cousin the coyote, a.k.a. the "songdog"—howl for a bewildering variety of reasons: to communicate to other members of the pack, to signal their location, to proclaim the end of the day, to welcome the dawn, to greet the moon, and to express the entire gamut of emotions, from great joy to deep sorrow, enormous loneliness to profound contentment. Beyond a certain point, though, I don't think there's much to be gained by dissecting the root cause of howling. I mean, do a pub full of Irishmen need a reason to sing?

WHY ARE PUPPIES BORN "DEAF?"

Essentially, it's for the same reason that they're born "blind." (And yes, I know they're not really born deaf—although some puppies are—but it gets a little tiresome saying "born unable to hear because their ear canals are closed.") Over the eons, the strategy that worked best for the wolf's survival, and therefore became integral to the dog's genetic make-up, was a gestation period of about two months followed by a two-week "neo-natal" period during which many features of the puppies' physiology undergo critical development—development that the young of more precocious species (the large hooved mammals, for example) undergo while still in the womb.

A certain amount of sensory deprivation is an important part of this process. Just as the puppy's eyelids are fused shut to protect the nascent optic structures until they're ready to respond to light, the pup's ear canals are sealed closed, thus preventing sound waves from entering and "activating" the fragile auditory machinery until it, too, is capable of handling the stimulus. Unlike the sense of sight, however, which starts out at a very rudimentary level and grows in acuity over the weeks that follow, the puppy's sense of hearing is quite acute as soon as the ear canals fully open.

WHY DO DOGS PANT?

Dogs pant for some of the same reasons we do. For example, the anticipation of a pleasurable experience—for dogs, feeding time, going for a walk, being hitched to a sled—often leads to excited panting. Dogs also pant, obviously, in response to exertion. But the biggest reason dogs pant is that it's their primary means of dissipating heat and staying cool—in other words, regulating their body temperature. By rapidly moving air across the membranes in their mouths, moisture is evaporated. And as you recall from high-school physics, the process of evaporation draws off heat, thus cooling the affected surface. The same principle is at work when people sweat; it's just the mechanism that's different.

For the record, dogs do sweat—through the pads of their feet—but to such a negligible extent that canine physiologists dismiss the dog's sweat glands as "rudimentary" and "essentially non-functional." The problem with panting as a means of staying cool is that sometimes a dog simply can't keep up, particularly when high ambient temperature is coupled with high relative humidity. Once a dog's body temperature creeps above 104°F (the upper end of normal is 102°), heatstroke—or worse—becomes a distinct possibility. This is why no conscientious person ever confines a dog in a car during hot weather. It's a tragedy waiting to happen.

WHY DO PUPPIES' MOTHERS CLEAN UP AFTER THEM FOR THE FIRST FEW WEEKS—AND WHY DO THEY STOP?

One of the measures of how helpless puppies are at birth—and how utterly reliant they are on their mothers—is that they can't even defecate or urinate on their own. Instead, by licking their anuses and uro-genital openings, the puppies' dam stimulates them to poop and pee. This continues for approximately two to three weeks, when the pups, despite their wobbly legs, begin "taking care of business" by themselves. During this same neo-natal period and for some time beyond, the mother also cleans up after her puppies, dutifully hoovering their soft, relatively odorless (or at least not terribly malodorous) stools. This is nature's way of keeping the whelping and brooding area clean, thus minimizing its attraction both to parasites and potential predators. In that place deep in the dog's psyche where the wolf still howls, mama wants her nest to be as inconspicuous as possible.

Once the pups start eating solid food, though, their stools become unpalatable and the dam grows increasingly disinclined to "police the area." This has the effect of kick-starting the weaning process, and as milk comprises an ever-smaller percentage of the pups' diet the bitch produces less and less of it until she finally "dries up." The pups, in turn, are forced to become more independent and assert their individuality—putting them in just the right place, psychologically, to start new lives with their human pack.

WHY DO PUPPIES "SPIN" LIKE WIND-UP TOYS?

In a way, this question has it backwards. It seems entirely likely to me that, in yet another instance of art imitating life, spinning puppies were the inspiration that caused wind-up toys to be invented in the first place. It would be closer to the truth, then, to say that wind-up toys spin like puppies.

So why do puppies spin? Because they're so excited, so exuberantly joyful, so overcome by the delirious thrill of living and the possibilities of their existence that, if they could, they'd come right out of their skins. They literally don't know what to do with themselves, but somehow, someway, they have to move. It's like the way some people just have to dance when they hear Tina Turner sing "Proud Mary." Another factor that influences and even conditions pups to spin (as opposed to racing back-and-forth, another common expression of youthful exuberance) is that they're in a relatively small space—the whelping pen, for example. Their options are limited, and spinning gives them the biggest bang for their buck. There's a demonstrative aspect as well. Having learned to associate people with good things—food, play, etc.— there's a sense in which the pups spin for you. And even older dogs will spin circles in anticipation of suppertime, going for a walk, or some other pleasant experience.

A certain amount of happy, situational spinning is normal—but chronic, excessive spinning is often the sign of a pup that's spent too much time confined to a crate and is poorly socialized in general. It can also be symptomatic of a serious underlying neurological condition—epilepsy, to name one—so if your pup's spinning to a degree that causes concern, a visit to the veterinarian is definitely in order.

WHY DO DOGS IN PARKED CARS TEND TO GROWL AND BARE THEIR TEETH?

One of the few hard-and-fast rules governing human-canine interaction is that you should never, ever, under any circumstances approach a strange dog that's shut in a car. (With the possible exception of a dog that's obviously in trouble because its moron owner shut it in on a hot day and didn't crack the windows.) This is why police vehicles assigned to "K-9" units have stern "Stay Back!" warnings printed on them.

Leaving a dog in a car brings out the most extreme form of its sense of territoriality. In the dog's mind, it's been charged with the duty of defending the property of the "pack," not to mention itself and its own "space." The dog is also put in the proverbial back-against-the-wall position, with nowhere to run and nowhere to hide should it be confronted by an aggressor it would normally flee from. The upshot is that it feels compelled to make a display of force at even the remotest suggestion of a threat—and it construes its threats very broadly. (Frankly, it's not a great idea to approach a strange dog in any situation without the consent and facilitation of its owner. In dogs as in people, looks can be deceiving.)

WHY DO DOGS RISK THEIR LIVES TO SAVE THEIR MASTERS?

The lore and literature of dogdom is replete with tales of canine courage, selflessness and sacrifice: the duck hunter whose boat capsizes in a snowstorm, only to be towed to shore by grasping the tail of the Labrador that swims in circles around him, refusing to leave his side; the child knocked out of the path of a speeding car by the mutt her parents rescued from the animal shelter; the family saved from asphyxiation by the cocker spaniel that wouldn't stop barking and scratching at the bedroom door until someone got up to investigate, then discovered the first insidious tendrils of smoke wisping up from the floorboards. Dogs have pulled people from the burning wreckage of cars and buildings and fought to repulse violent intruders even after suffering mortal wounds.

Dogs have stayed with people who would have frozen to death without their warmth or summoned help when their masters suffered injuries far from civilization.

Little wonder that the dog, from the beginning of recorded history, has been considered the very exemplar of loyalty, embodying this quality to a degree we rarely find in ourselves. You could argue that the reason dogs perform these selfless acts is that they have no foreknowledge of death, and are thus unburdened by the free-floating fears and anxieties that so profoundly influence human behavior. Personally, I prefer to believe that dogs do such things because, despite their flaws, faults and idiosyncrasies, they are the finest and most inherently noble beings on the face of this earth.

WHY DO KENNELED DOGS PACE ALL DAY?

They don't; they pace just long enough to lay a colossal guilt trip on you for not giving them more exercise, free play, field work, whatever. In dogs as in humans, pacing is a kind of pressure valve for the release of pent-up nervous energy, which explains why breeds that tend to be high-strung—field-bred pointers and English setters, for example—are also champion pacers.

It's likely, too, that it's an expression of the natural wanderlust common to the canid race, what Elizabeth Marshall Thomas, in her acclaimed *The Hidden Life of Dogs,* refers to as the desire for "voyaging." All creatures have daily (and seasonal) rhythms, and there are times when a dog simply needs to stretch its legs. Unable to hunt or voyage, the kenneled dog paces. The good news is that the confirmed pacer gives itself what amounts to a self-pedicure, meaning you don't have to clip its toenails very often.

WHY DO DOGS COME IN SO MANY SIZES, SHAPES, AND COLORS?

No species exhibits a greater degree of what scientists call "morphological variability" than the dog. It strains the imagination to look at a tiny, two-pound Chihuahua and a massive, 180-pound Saint Bernard and believe that they share the same basic genetic blueprint. Indeed, what's perhaps even more amazing than the dog's incredible range of physical variation is how little dogs vary at their most fundamental level. There are no genetic "markers," for example, that enable scientists to distinguish one breed from another. All appearances to the contrary, low-slung Dachshunds and towering Irish wolfhounds are more alike than different. The same goes for needle-nosed collies and scrunch-faced pugs, elegant Afghans and lumbering bulldogs, or any other pairing of opposites you can dream up from among the 400-plus breeds presently roaming the earth. (It's thought that as many as 1,000 distinct breeds have existed at one time or another.)

To account for the dog's diversity of sizes, shapes, colors, etc., you have only to consider that the species has been domesticated for 15,000 years—longer than any other animal—and that throughout this period humans have selectively bred it to display and embody characteristics they find useful, admirable, and attractive. It takes no great leap to grasp the enormity of the possibilities. The breeds we have today are their living proof.

WHY DO HOUNDS FOLLOW TRACKS?

There's no doubt that one of the earliest functions of the dog was to help human hunters locate, track, and recover game animals that were relied upon for food. It was simply a matter of harnessing and directing the dog's natural predatory instincts—letting it "follow its nose," so to speak. And that, essentially, is what hounds do. The development of bona fide "scent" hounds seems to have begun about 2,500 years ago in classical Greece, and was in full swing by the time the Romans first described the bloodhound in the third century AD. Medieval writers on sport list a bewildering variety of hounds—lymers, alaunts, etc.—each of which was prized for the unique talents it brought to the hunt of the stag or the boar, the principal quarry of antiquity. The word "quarry," in fact, derives from a French term for the ritual distribution of tidbits from slain prey to the dogs that participated in its capture.

In the lexicon of the houndsman, a "cold nose" refers not to the way a dog's nose feels against your skin, but to its ability to pick up a "cold"—as in not fresh—trail. This is an extremely important quality in bloodhounds, which are often used to find people lost in remote areas or to track down fugitives from justice. In hounds used for sport, however—coon hounds, foxhounds, beagles—a nose that's too cold can be a liability. There's a fine line between an exciting hunt and a wild goose chase, and a dog that "strikes" or "opens"—that is, gives tongue—on old scent tends to precipitate the latter.

WHY DO DOGS NAP SO OFTEN?

This question, I think, betrays a certain cultural bias. By American standards, yes, dogs take frequent naps. But in America sleeplessness—or, more precisely, the ability to function without sleep—is seen as a badge of honor. Instead of emulating the custom of more advanced nations and indulging in regular siestas, we gulp coffee, pop No-Doz, and generally do whatever it takes to stay awake when the civilized choice would be to recline, relax, and check our eyelids for leaks. It's almost as if we consider the nap somehow morally offensive, a reflection of deep, dark failings. There's also the vividly imagined fear that if we take a nap, the competition—whoever or whatever that might me—will get the drop on us.

Blissfully unencumbered by such baggage (or by the various other demons that plague the late-20th century American mind), the dog with nothing better to do and all its basic needs satisfied settles in for a snooze. Unlike us, dogs don't fight their nature. If it feels good, and the laws of the "pack" don't prohibit it, they do it. And, as Elizabeth Marshall Thomas observed, dogs relish the opportunity to simply "do nothing."

WHY ARE DOGS DISTRUSTFUL OF SOME STRANGERS AND NOT OTHERS?

While it's very politically correct to own a dog—and, from what I've read lately, a great way for single people to get dates—dogs themselves are very politically incorrect. They are unrepentant and irremediable stereotypers, drop-outs from Logic 101 who persist in falling into the trap of inductive reasoning. Which is to say, if a dog has a bad experience with a cigar-smoking man wearing sunglasses and a dark, three-piece suit, it's going to view every person who fits this description with deep suspicion. This is why, again, it's always a good idea, when you're meeting a dog for the first time, to have the owner facilitate the introduction. For all you know, the dog could have been mistreated by someone who used the same aftershave that you do, and, as the saying goes, once bitten, twice shy.

In the wild, obviously, where giving the benefit of the doubt tends to have a negative effect on one's longevity, this trait makes a lot of sense. There is very little survival value in regarding a lion, for example, as an individual rather than as a representative of a certain class. Again, this is an area in which some observers believe that dogs are able to "sense" the evil that lurks in the hearts of men. The more likely explanation is that a person with bad intentions telegraphs them in subtle ways that dogs, being keen observers, pick up on even when we don't. Unfortunately, dogs are not infallible in this respect, as many postal service employees are painfully aware.

WHY DO DOGS BEG FOR FOOD?

Setting aside the question of whether or not dogs should even get table scraps, it would be hard to cite a more clear-cut example of the power of positive reinforcement—which is to say, dogs beg for food because it's a tactic that works. The desired result—a morsel of the good stuff on your plate—is achieved. Over time, of course, each dog perfects its individual style in this regard, from the classic "sit up and beg" posture to the nudge-and-whimper, the sad, discomfiting stare, the muzzle-on-the-thigh, and various unbearably irresistible permutations thereof. An English setter of my acquaintance not only sits up and begs, but crosses his forepaws when he does so. Needless to say, his prowess as a panhandler is legendary.

Some dogs even learn that the best way to beg for food is to pretend not to, and that the probability of reward increases markedly by feigning complete indifference. Don't be fooled: These sharps know exactly what they're doing.

WHY DOES PUPPY BREATH SMELL SO SWEET?

The mere fact that you're reading this means you're a puppy-lover, so I really shouldn't have to convince you that puppy breath is an exhalation of such divine and wondrous subtlety that there is literally nothing to compare it to. It's a kind of vaporous nectar, a misty swirl of milk and honey, and you don't smell it so much as you drink it, savoring every draught to the last delicious molecule. It's addictive, narcotic, and if you need further proof just Google "puppy breath." What you'll find is a vast community of zealots, ordained by the force of their beliefs to extol the miracle that is puppy breath and share it with the rest of the world. It's a bit alarming, really.

The reason puppy breath smells the way it does—sweet but not cloyingly so, like a warm summer breeze wafting through a peach orchard—is that the puppy's diet of mother's milk, along with the enzymes that break it down, combine in what can only be described as alchemy. The result is singular—and magical. But it is also, like puppyhood itself, ephemeral. As the puppy is weaned and milk comprises an ever-smaller percentage of its diet, its breath gradually changes to, well, dog breath. By the time the pup's three months of age, the breath that made you want to hold it to your face at every opportunity has all but vanished. It's not that dog breath's bad, necessarily (although the breath of a dog with periodontal disease or a throat abcess will send you reeling), it's just that the only dogs with good breath tend to be yours. Funny how that works.

WHY DO PUPPIES HAVE THAT SPECIAL "PUPPY SMELL?"

Like the aroma of baking bread, or the scent of cotton sheets hung out to dry on the first warm day of spring, puppies have a smell that's all their own—and that's hard to get enough of. A certain portion of this is attributable to the phenomenon of "puppy breath" which, if it could be distilled, bottled, and sold would make some entrepreneur very, very rich. Another factor is the fastidious grooming performed by the puppy's mother, who starts licking them as soon as they exit the birth canal—it's pretty comical to watch a tiny newborn pup get rolled across the whelping box like a bocce ball—and maintains this practice until they're well on their way to being weaned. (You'd smell good, too, if you had someone willing to bathe you every three or four hours.) It's also the case that, in somewhat the same way that teenage kids begin having skin problems when they reach puberty, the oily secretions called sebum don't fully kick in until around six months of age (it varies from breed to breed), when the pup begins to shed its "puppy coat" and grow in its adult coat. These secretions, which are produced by glands in the hair follicles and are what give the coat its gloss and sheen, are the primary source of "dog smell," at least as far as the dull olfactory powers of humans are concerned. Other dogs, of course, find the scent emitted by their brethren's anal sacs to be much more instructive.

In any event, enjoy your puppy's smell while you can, because it'll be gone before you can say "Get off the couch!"

WHY DO DOGS LIKE TO HANG THEIR HEADS OUT THE CAR WINDOW?

et's clear the air right now and stress that, unless you're prepared to equip him with goggles, this really isn't a good thing to let your dog do. Neither is letting your dog ride loose in the back of the pickup, a practice that strikes me as the equivalent of riding a motorcycle without a helmet: It's fine—until it isn't.

Beyond the fact that the average image-conscious dog looks major cool with his ears flapping in the wind and a silly grin on his face (the envy of all his kenneled, fenced-in, and otherwise tethered brethren), I think the answer lies in those 220 million scent receptors stuffed inside his snout. A dog's sense of smell is its primary means of apprehending its world, a world that, given our own pitiful olfactory powers, we can scarcely imagine. And a dog shut up inside a car experiences the same kind of sensory deprivation you and I would if we were locked inside a darkened room. So when it sticks its head out the window, it's essentially flipping on the floodlights. Even when the window's barely rolled down, the typical dog will wedge his nose into the crack—just to see what is going on out there.

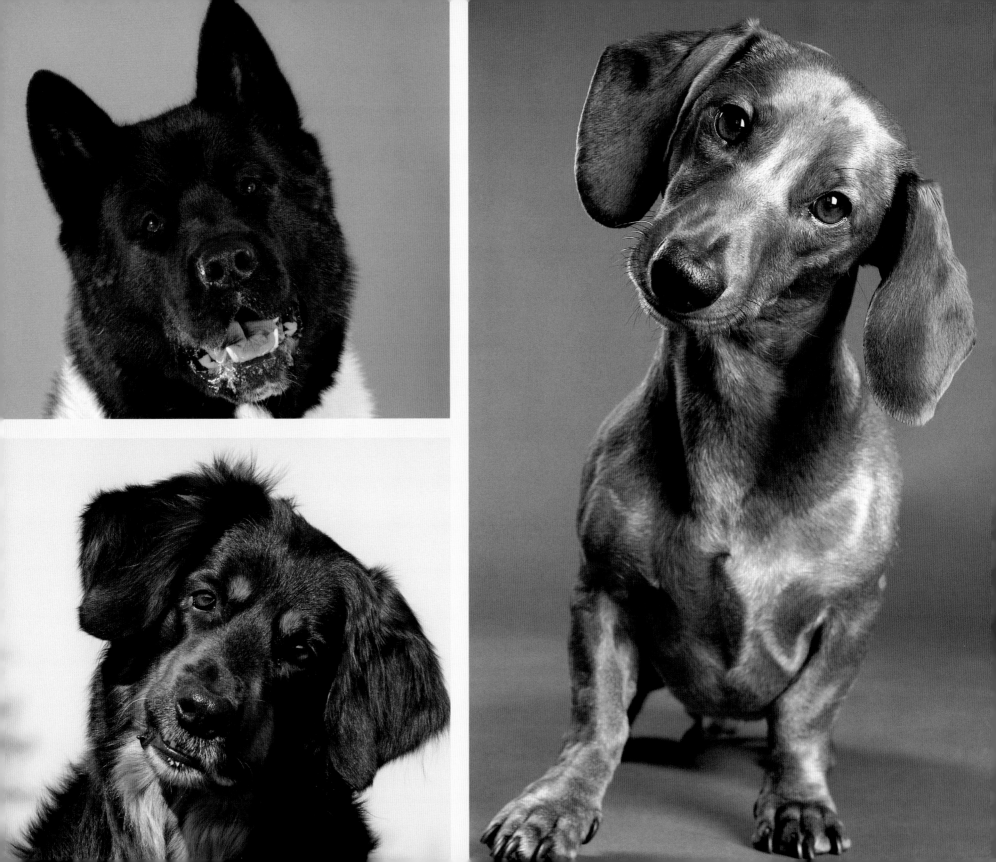

WHY DO DOGS SEEM TO UNDERSTAND AND RESPOND TO OUR MOODS?

t's often said that dogs can "sense" our moods, and no one who's spent any amount of time in their company would dispute this. Dogs are great empathizers, able not only to tune in to our emotional wavelength, but to give us precisely what we need: a boisterous greeting, a soulful, knowing gaze, a reassuring thump of the tail. If more people had dogs, there would be far fewer of what are known generically as "mental health professionals." Indeed, the therapeutic value of canine companionship, especially for those who are elderly, disabled, or alone, is well-documented; simply put, people who have dogs tend to be happier than those who don't.

Some observers, at a loss to explain the extraordinary insights of which dogs are capable, have credited them with a kind of ESP—a "sixth sense," if you will. There's actually a germ of truth in this contention: Dogs, after all, can hear things we can't (hence the so-called "silent" whistle), and the world revealed to them by their noses is as brilliant, distinct, and variegated as our world of sight. Given the fact that emotional turmoil is often expressed physiologically, it's not a stretch to argue that dogs can, on occasion, literally smell our moods. Think of it this way: If people can "smell fear" (as the PIs in detective novels always seem to do), dogs certainly can. Dogs are also masters at reading body language and picking up on subtle inflections of voice, manner, and carriage. You could almost say that they know us better than we know ourselves.

WHY DO WET DOGS ALWAYS SHAKE ON YOU?

This is one of those Law of Nature deals that defies logical explanation. The day you sell your stock is the day before a takeover bid doubles its price, when you discover a restaurant you really like it promptly goes belly-up... You get the picture. I suppose it could be argued that dogs shake on you because (A) they're not especially pleased at getting wet and they want you to know it, or (B) they're having so much fun in the water that they want to spread the happiness around. It could be, too, that they're so focused on the task at hand—retrieving a duck, for example—that they simply forget, and it doesn't even occur to them to shake until the job is finished. By then, of course, we're talking point-blank range.

WHY DO POINTING BREED PUPPIES "SIGHT POINT" AT A VERY EARLY AGE?

It never fails to produce "oohs," "aahs," and "wows"—an entire litter of pudgy, shoebox-sized puppies frozen in their tracks, their tails rigid (as rigid as they can make them, anyway) and their expressions deadly serious as they sight-point a robin, or a butterfly, or, most likely, a pheasant, grouse, or quail wing flicked from an old fishing rod. Although it doesn't have to be a wing—a white handkerchief, or anything else that gets and keeps the pups' attention, works just as well—the "wing on a string" is a time-honored tool for assessing a puppy's pointing instinct. A pup that readily locks up on the wing is said to have "a lot of point," and is generally considered a better, more precocious prospect than a pup that just wants to chase it. Many experienced dog people are also convinced that the style and intensity a puppy displays while pointing a wing accurately predict the style and intensity it will display as an adult.

This is one of those behaviors that's directly attributable to hundreds of years of selective breeding. First the point itself, which has its roots in the stalk common to all mammalian predators, was isolated and "fixed"—a process that began as early as the 13th century. Then, as it was continually refined and reinforced, it became the dominant, definitive behavior of the pointer (the acknowledged top dog in this respect), the setters, and, to a somewhat lesser extent, the other pointing breeds. Some pups start pointing by the time they're three weeks old—as soon as their legs work and their eyes are open, basically.

WHY DO PUPPIES GET THE HICCUPS?

Most of us have had the experience, notoriously recreated in an episode of Seinfeld, of being introduced by beaming parents to their newborn pride-and-joy… and recoiling in shock at the face peeking up from the crib. This is when the ability to display "grace under pressure," in Hemingway's famous formulation, goes a long way.

Happily, we don't have to worry about this with puppies. They can be sort of lumpy and amorphous, even amoeboid, during their first few weeks of life, but they're never unappealing. Something that puppies and babies do have in common, though, is that they both get the hiccups. Getting the hiccups is natural and normal—kind of endearing in fact (human babies even get hiccups in utero)—and while eating, drinking, and general excitement can sometimes trigger an "attack" there's often no discernible rhyme or reason to them. The good news is that they tend to pass just as quickly and unaccountably as they started—and no, you should not try to "scare" the hiccups out of a puppy, or for that matter attempt any of the other home remedies that your mom may have inflicted on you when it seemed your hiccups would never subside. Most puppies outgrow the hiccups by the time they're eight months old or so, and while an older dog will occasionally get them there seems to be no record of canine hiccups lasting for years and even decades, as has been documented in humans. As for the question of why hiccups happen in the first place, there's some speculation that they may have originally aided in dislodging food that was "stuck," but the bottom line is that no one really knows.

WHY DO DOGS PREFER OTHER DOGS' FOOD TO THEIR OWN—EVEN WHEN IT'S EXACTLY THE SAME?

Dogs are no different from kids in this respect. Children always seem to have a sneaking suspicion that they're getting the shaft, that their brother/sister/friend has a sweeter deal than they do. And even when you offer hard, objective proof to the contrary, they still believe, secretly, that the other kid not only has more of it—whatever "it" may be—but

that it's bigger, better, and altogether cooler, too. This is why, if you place identical bowls of kibble in front of dogs occupying adjacent runs and leave the gates open, chances are they'll trade places in about two shakes of their tails. No doubt the dog's innate "food-competitiveness" (see also #25) plays a role in triggering this behavior as well.

WHY DO DOGS EAT GRASS?

Remember, dogs are carnivores by nature, but omnivores by necessity. And by circumstance: When wolves bring down a moose, deer, caribou, or any of the other large herbivores that comprise the bulk of their diet, they immediately tear into its paunch, consuming not only the flesh and organs but vegetable matter in various states of digestion. The dog's desire for an occasional salad, therefore, is an atavistic expression of its racial memory, a harking back to the ways of its ancestors. And despite the "balanced nutrition" provided by most dog foods these days, there's something about a side of fresh greens (especially, it seems, in the springtime) that's awfully tempting. It could be the flavor, it could be the texture—no one really knows.

The problem is that the digestive system of the dog isn't well-equipped to handle the stuff "straight" (not partially pre-digested), which is why there's often a direct cause-and-effect relationship between grass-eating and upchucking. In fact, dogs suffering from an upset stomach will eat grass specifically to induce vomiting, hoping to purge whatever ill humors are affecting them.

WHY DO PUPPIES SLEEP ON THEIR BACKS?

Whether '70s punk-rock pioneers The Ramones originated the phrase or merely appropriated it for their album of the same name, "bop 'til you drop" has become part of the American vernacular. ("Shop 'til you drop" came later, presumably.) And while certain nuances of meaning tend to be lost in translation, it basically means to keep going at full speed until your legs can't support you any more and you literally collapse on the spot from exhaustion. If this m.o. sounds familiar, it's because it describes puppies, up to the age of three or four months or so to the proverbial T. They go, and go, and go until, as you watch with a growing smile, they wobble, totter, and fall. You're tempted to holler "Timber!"

So it's not so much that they specifically sleep on their backs as it is that they sleep—soundly, comfortably, and deeply—in whatever position, and in whatever location they happen to be in. This is an ability that many Americans, by all accounts the world's most troubled sleepers, can only envy (as they reach for their Ambien). Some adult dogs occasionally sleep on their backs as well, which is if anything an even more comical sight than the puppy version. Come to think of it, all the adult dogs I've known to sleep on their backs were males. I suppose this could be evidence of a streak of exhibitionism, but I'll let you draw your own conclusions.

WHY DO DOGS WALK IN A CIRCLE BEFORE LYING DOWN?

Robert Benchley, the acerbic humorist and unofficial chairman of the Adirondack Round Table, argued that one of the reasons a boy should have a dog is that "it teaches him to turn around three times before lying down." The "why" of this, however, has received surprisingly little attention from students of canine behavior. Folklore has it that dogs circle to flush out any snakes that might be lurking in the area. Given the fact that a snake-bitten dog of yore was unlikely to enjoy the opportunity to procreate, this explanation has a certain rough-hewn Darwinian logic.

A somewhat more plausible (albeit less colorful) theory, though, is that wolves circled in order to flatten the vegetation and simply make themselves more comfortable. Over the eons, this behavior became incorporated at the genetic level. The really interesting question (one that strikes me as the kind the late Ed Zern loved to ponder in his wonderful "Exit, Laughing" column in Field & Stream) is whether or not dogs in the northern and southern hemispheres, respectively, circle in different directions as a result of the Coriolis Effect.

WHY DO SLED DOGS PULL?

The Romans used a large, mastiff-type dog called a "molossus" as a draft animal; that is, an animal used to "draw" a load. And there's no doubt that dogs had been similarly employed for thousands of years by the time the Romans got around to writing about it. The breeds known collectively as "sled dogs"—the malamute, Samoyed, Siberian husky, etc.—are derived from the dogs used by indigenous Arctic tribes, although there is some debate in the anthropological camp as to when these peoples actually became mushers. Interestingly, the "Alaskan husky"—the dog that professional sled-dog racers, such as those who compete in the Iditarod, use almost exclusively—is not a recognized breed at all. Rather, it is a continuously evolving genre, a dog bred and developed not according to an arbitrary standard of appearance, but to a rigorous standard of performance. What is important is not the pedigree, but the contribution the individual dog can make in the way of increased speed, endurance, trainability, and/or leadership.

Unlike pointing or retrieving, behaviors that can be viewed as refinements to the dog's basic prey drive, pulling probably originated as something dogs were simply taught to do, something suited to their physical and mental constitutions. Over the millennia, as the dogs exhibiting the most ability in this regard were selectively bred, the sled dog "type" emerged. The fact of the matter, though, is that many dogs, regardless of breed, just seem to get a kick out of pulling.

WHY DO DOGS LICK PEOPLE? ARE THEY KISSING US?

t's either that they are kissing you, or a cheap ploy to clean up the blueberry muffin crumbs clinging to your chin. Personally, I happen to think that it is a dog's way of kissing, at least insofar as kissing can be broadly defined as any oral display of affection. And because most of us react with delight—or at least all true dog lovers do—we reinforce the behavior. What I find interesting is the variety of styles, from the frenzied, slobbery, rapid-fire approach to the slow, solemn measured one.

Zack, my English setter previously mentioned, was not big on showing affection.

But whenever I'd let him ride in the front seat of the truck, he'd sit facing me, gravely look me in the eye for a moment or two, and then, starting at my chin and ending at the tip of my nose, give me one tender, deliberate lick. Never two, always and only one. Then, feeling that he'd expressed as much emotion as the moment warranted, he'd curl up on the seat, using my thigh as a pillow for his unutterably lovely head. God, how I miss that dog.

WHY DO DOGS LOVE TO CHEW SLIPPERS?

A little review seems to be in order here. We've established the fact that dogs like to chew; we've also established that they're peculiarly attracted to things of a somewhat "ripe" nature. Add these proclivities together, and it's easy to understand why a slipper, high with the Limburger smell of foot odor, is such a tempting target.

The average slipper also happens to fit quite comfortably into the mouth of the average dog. The texture and consistency are appealing, too, especially if the slipper's made of deerskin or a good, supple leather. Dogs enjoy chewing gloves for the same reasons; indeed, several highly regarded professional trainers use an old leather glove to encourage puppies to retrieve. Of course, it's impossible to mention dogs and slippers without recalling the classic, Rockwellian image of the man who, following a hard day at the office, returns home, settles into his easy chair, and bids his doting canine to fetch his pipe and slipper.

WHY ARE PUPPIES SO IRRESISTIBLE—AND WHY DO THEY ALWAYS MAKE US SO HAPPY?

I was going to talk about the 15,000 years (if not longer) that we've shared our homes and hearths with dogs, about the intricate workings of symbiosis and the mysteries of co-evolution, about how we've made the dog not in our own image but in the image of our idealized selves, the people we wish we were. I was going to talk about the way they know us better than we know ourselves, too, about their uncanny ability to tune into our emotional wavelength and give us what we need to get by. I was going to talk about our shared capacities for love and play, about loyalty and tolerance and faithfulness and all the other noble qualities the dog possesses, and I was going to make the argument that we have a kind of innate attraction to puppies, a bred-in-the-bone receptivity to everything they embody and represent.

But then I thought, "Come on." You might as well ask why the sun comes up, or why water is wet, or why the stars glitter in the night sky. If you want to know why puppies are irresistible, and why they make us happy, all you need to do is spend, oh, about two seconds in their swirling, squirming, frolicking company. There are realms words cannot illuminate, and the place puppies occupy in the human heart is one of them.

WHY DO GREYHOUNDS RACE?

Greyhounds belong to a class of dogs known as "sight hounds" or, more poetically, "gazehounds." By either name, it refers to a dog developed to run down visually targeted prey in open country (as opposed to "scent" hounds that rely almost entirely on their noses and rarely, if ever, sight their prey before it is brought to bay). The gazehound was, in all likelihood, the first dog bred for a specific purpose, and thus the first true breed. Dogs remarkably similar in appearance to the Saluki are depicted in 5,000-year-old Egyptian tomb paintings. The Saluki, of course, is essentially a greyhound with feathers (feathers in this sense being the long hair on the ears, tail, and legs). And, a smooth-coated dog fitting the greyhound profile to the proverbial T

was described by the Roman poet, Ovid, at about the same time that a carpenter's son was beginning to stir things up in Galilee. It's probable, in fact, that the Romans originally brought the greyhound to England, where, over the centuries, the sport of "coursing" emerged as a means to determine who had the fastest dog.

In the 20th century, the mechanical "bunny" replaced the live hare, and greyhound racing as we know it was born. All of which is a roundabout way of explaining that greyhounds race because they have been bred for thousands of years to have a burning desire to chase things, and to be endowed with the blazing speed necessary to catch them.

WHY DO DOGS STEAL OUR HEARTS?

Does the phrase "beyond redemption" mean anything to you? Dogs steal our hearts because they touch us in ways that nothing else does, and in places that nothing else can reach. They move us with their courage, loyalty, and resolve; they astound us with their athletic prowess and the awesome capabilities of their noses; they delight us with their playfulness and eagerness-to-please; they comfort us with their uncanny ability to peer into our souls.

The bond between dogs and people has been forged by 15,000 years of mutual admiration and mutual trust. Civilizations have risen and fallen, the terrifying unknown has been explored, the great obstacles to human progress surmounted. And it has all been done with the dog—partner, companion, protector—at our side. Dogs don't steal our hearts; we surrendered our hearts to them long, long ago